마가복음 쓰기를 시작하며

마가복음 쓰기를 시작한 이유와 쓰고 난 후 기대하는 점 등을 기록해 보세요.

시작한 날

년. 월. 일.

십대를 위한
마가복음
영어로 한 달 쓰기
ESV®

일러두기

성경 본문은 Crossway가 발행한 The Holy Bible Standard Version(ESV)를 사용했습니다.

하루 한 장, 지혜가 트이고 공부습관이 잡힌다

십대를 위한
마가복음
영어로 한 달 쓰기 ESV®

사랑플러스 편집부 엮음

사랑플러스

성경 쓰기,
하나님의 지혜와 통하는 길

'나는 앞으로 무엇을 하면서 살아야 할까?'
'공부가 너무 힘들어. 어떻게 하면 잘할 수 있을까?'
'친구들이 나를 싫어하면 어쩌지?'
'부모님이 나 때문에 실망하시지는 않을까?'

답답하고 불안한 마음을 달래기 위해 스마트폰으로 친구들과 수다를 떨기도 하고, 코노(코인 노래방)에서 목청껏 노래도 해 보고, 게임에 빠져들기도 하지만 좀처럼 마음을 다잡을 수 없습니다.

우리는 이렇게 고민되는 순간을 수없이 마주하며 살아갑니다. 매번 어려운 선택의 기로에 놓이기도 하지요. 그때마다 우리는 무엇이 옳은 선택인지, 내가 과연 잘하고 있는 것인지 헷갈리기만 합니다. 누군가 '이럴 땐 이렇게 하고, 저럴 땐 저렇게 해야 한다'는 명확한 기준을 제시해 주면 좋겠다는 생각이 듭니다.

그렇다면 우리는 어떻게 중요한 일을 결정하고, 바른 선택을 할 수 있을까요? 해답은 바로 '지혜'에 있어요. 지혜는 바른 판단력과 분별력을 제공해 주는 보물과 같습니다. 지혜로운 사람이 되면 하나님이 원하시는 것이 무엇인지, 나를 향한 계획은 무엇인지 찾을 수 있어요. 하지만 지혜가 없으면 자기도 모르게 죄에 빠질 수 있고, 심지어 하나님을 떠나기도 해요.

그렇다면 지혜는 어떻게 얻을 수 있을까요? 하나님의 말씀인 성경이 바로 지혜가 가득 담긴 보물 창고입니다. 성경을 읽고 묵상하다 보면 '어떻게 사는 것이 잘 사는 인생'인지 명확하게 알 수 있지요.

읽기만 하면 될걸 귀찮고 시간도 없는데 왜 굳이 손으로 써야 할까요? 성경을 한 글자, 한 글자 천천히 따라 쓰다 보면 생각하는 시간이 생기기 때문에 말씀이 손과 머리 그리고 가슴 깊숙한 곳까지 뻗어 내려오는 걸 느낄 수 있어요. 중요한 말씀이 눈으로 슥 지나가지 않고 개념 하나하나가 생생하게 와닿는 경험을 할 수 있을 거예요. 뿐만 아니라 글을 잘 쓸 수 있는 능력이 생겨요. 좋은 문장을 따라 쓰면서 나도 모르는 사이에 어휘력과 문장력이 향상된답니다.

자, 이제 무궁무진한 지혜의 바다로 항해를 시작해 볼까요?

마가복음

마가복음은 흔히 네 개의 복음서(마태복음, 마가복음, 누가복음, 요한복음) 중에 가장 먼저 쓰인 복음서로 알려져 있습니다. 또 마가복음은 '행동의 복음'이라 불리기도 하는데, 그 이유는 이 복음서에 나오는 사건들이 빠르게 움직이기 때문입니다. 네 개의 복음서 중 내용은 가장 짧지만 복음의 핵심들이 응축되어 있습니다. 한편, 마가복음은 예수님의 표정과 몸짓 같은 자세한 사항들을 상세히 묘사함으로 그 당시의 사건을 생동감 있게 전달해줍니다.

마가복음의 안내를 따라 예수님의 길을 함께 걷다 보면 이 땅의 구원자로 오신 예수님의 완전하신 사랑과 은혜, 그리고 그분이 선포하신 진리의 말씀을 깨닫게 됩니다. 그리고 그로 말미암아 진리 안에서 풍성한 기쁨을 누리게 될 것입니다.

DAY 1

DATE . . .

Mark 1

John the Baptist Prepares the Way

1 The beginning of the gospel of Jesus Christ, the Son of God.

2 As it is written in Isaiah the prophet, "Behold, I send my
messenger before your face, who will prepare your way,

3 the voice of one crying in the wilderness: 'Prepare the way of
the Lord, make his paths straight,'"

4 John appeared, baptizing in the wilderness and proclaiming
a baptism of repentance for the forgiveness of sins.

5 And all the country of Judea and all Jerusalem were going out
to him and were being baptized by him in the river Jordan,
confessing their sins.

6 Now John was clothed with camel's hair and wore a leather belt
around his waist and ate locusts and wild honey.

7 And he preached, saying, "After me comes he who is mightier
than I, the strap of whose sandals I am not worthy to stoop down
and untie.

8 I have baptized you with water, but he will baptize you with
the Holy Spirit."

The Baptism of Jesus

9 In those days Jesus came from Nazareth of Galilee and was baptized by John in the Jordan.

10 And when he came up out of the water, immediately he saw the heavens being torn open and the Spirit descending on him like a dove.

11 And a voice came from heaven, “You are my beloved Son; with you I am well pleased.”

The Temptation of Jesus

12 The Spirit immediately drove him out into the wilderness.

13 And he was in the wilderness forty days, being tempted by Satan. And he was with the wild animals, and the angels were ministering to him.

Jesus Begins His Ministry

14 Now after John was arrested*, Jesus came into Galilee, proclaiming the gospel of God,

15 and saying, “The time is fulfilled, and the kingdom of God is at hand; repent and believe in the gospel.”

Jesus Calls the First Disciples

16 Passing alongside the Sea of Galilee, he saw Simon and Andrew the brother of Simon casting a net into the sea, for they were fishermen.

* arrest [ərést] ⓢ 체포하다. ⓜ 체포, 저지.

17 And Jesus said to them, “Follow me, and I will make you become
fishers of men.”
18 And immediately they left their nets and followed him.
19 And going on a little farther, he saw James the son of Zebedee
and John his brother, who were in their boat mending* the nets.
20 And immediately he called them, and they left their father
Zebedee in the boat with the hired servants and followed him.

* mending [méndiŋ] ⑲ 수선. 수리물.

오늘의 외울 말씀

And Jesus said to them,
“Follow me, and I will make you become fishers of men.”
And immediately they left their nets and followed him. (1:17-18)

예수께서 이르시되
나를 따라오라 내가 너희로 사람을 낚는 어부가 되게 하리라 하시니
곧 그물을 버려 두고 따르니라.

하루 한 문장, 생각 쓰기

오늘 본문을 쓰면서 깨달은 지혜, 새롭게 다짐한 점,
떠오른 생각 등을 자유롭게 적어 보세요.

DAY 2

DATE . . .

Mark 1

Jesus Heals a Man with an Unclean Spirit

21 And they went into Capernaum, and immediately on the Sabbath
he entered the synagogue* and was teaching.

22 And they were astonished at his teaching, for he taught them as
one who had authority**, and not as the scribes.

23 And immediately there was in their synagogue a man with
an unclean spirit. And he cried out,

24 "What have you to do with us, Jesus of Nazareth? Have you come
to destroy us? I know who you are—the Holy One of God."

25 But Jesus rebuked him, saying, "Be silent, and come out of him!"

26 And the unclean spirit, convulsing him and crying out with
a loud voice, came out of him.

27 And they were all amazed, so that they questioned among
themselves, saying, "What is this? A new teaching with authority!
He commands even the unclean spirits, and they obey him."

28 And at once his fame spread everywhere throughout all
the surrounding region of Galilee.

* synagogue [sínəgɑ̀g] ⓜ 유대교 회당.

** authority [əθɔ́:rəti] ⓜ 권위. 권한. 지휘권.

Jesus Heals Many

29 And immediately he left the synagogue and entered the house of
Simon and Andrew, with James and John.

30 Now Simon's mother-in-law lay ill with a fever, and immediately
they told him about her.

31 And he came and took her by the hand and lifted her up, and
the fever left her, and she began to serve them.

32 That evening at sundown they brought to him all who were sick
or oppressed* by demons.

33 And the whole city was gathered together at the door.

34 And he healed many who were sick with various diseases,
and cast out many demons. And he would not permit
the demons to speak, because they knew him.

Jesus Preaches in Galilee

35 And rising very early in the morning, while it was still dark, he
departed and went out to a desolate** place, and there he prayed.

36 And Simon and those who were with him searched for him,

37 and they found him and said to him, "Everyone is looking for
you."

38 And he said to them, "Let us go on to the next towns, that I may
preach there also, for that is why I came out."

39 And he went throughout all Galilee, preaching in their
synagogues and casting out demons.

* oppressed [əprést] ⓗ 억압당하는, 탄압받는.

** desolate [désələt] ⓗ 황량한, 적막한. ⓢ 고적하게 만들다.

Jesus Cleanses a Leper

40 And a leper came to him, imploring him, and kneeling said to
him, "If you will, you can make me clean."

41 Moved with pity, he stretched out his hand and touched him
and said to him, "I will; be clean."

42 And immediately the leprosy* left him, and he was made clean.

43 And Jesus sternly charged him and sent him away at once,

44 and said to him, "See that you say nothing to anyone, but go,
show yourself to the priest and offer for your cleansing what
Moses commanded, for a proof** to them."

45 But he went out and began to talk freely about it, and to spread
the news, so that Jesus could no longer openly enter a town,
but was out in desolate places, and people were coming to him
from every quarter.

* leprosy [léprəsi] ⓜ 나병, 문둥병.

** proof [pru:f] ⓜ 입증, 증거. ⓗ 견디는.

오늘의 외울 말씀

Moved with pity, he stretched out his hand and touched him
and said to him, "I will; be clean."
And immediately the leprosy left him, and he was made clean. (1:41-42)

예수께서 불쌍히 여기사 손을 내밀어 그에게 대시며 이르시되
내가 원하노니 깨끗함을 받으라 하시니
곧 나병이 그 사람에게서 떠나가고 깨끗하여진지라.

하루 한 문장, 생각 쓰기

오늘 본문을 쓰면서 깨달은 지혜, 새롭게 다짐한 점,
떠오른 생각 등을 자유롭게 적어 보세요.

DAY 3

DATE . . .

Mark 2

Jesus Heals a Paralytic

1 And when he returned to Capernaum after some days, it was
reported that he was at home.

2 And many were gathered together, so that there was no more
room, not even at the door. And he was preaching the word to
them.

3 And they came, bringing to him a paralytic carried by four men.

4 And when they could not get near him because of the crowd,
they removed the roof above him, and when they had made
an opening, they let down the bed on which the paralytic lay.

5 And when Jesus saw their faith, he said to the paralytic,
"Son, your sins are forgiven."

6 Now some of the scribes were sitting there, questioning in their
hearts,

7 "Why does this man speak like that? He is blaspheming!
Who can forgive sins but God alone?"

8 And immediately Jesus, perceiving in his spirit that they thus
questioned within themselves, said to them, "Why do you
question these things in your hearts?

9 Which is easier, to say to the paralytic*, 'Your sins are forgiven,'
or to say, 'Rise, take up your bed and walk'?
10 But that you may know that the Son of Man has authority on
earth to forgive sins"—he said to the paralytic—
11 "I say to you, rise, pick up your bed, and go home."
12 And he rose and immediately picked up his bed and went out
before them all, so that they were all amazed and glorified God,
saying, "We never saw anything like this!"

Jesus Calls Levi

13 He went out again beside the sea, and all the crowd was coming
to him, and he was teaching them.
14 And as he passed by, he saw Levi the son of Alphaeus sitting at
the tax booth, and he said to him, "Follow me." And he rose and
followed him.
15 And as he reclined at table in his house, many tax collectors and
sinners were reclining with Jesus and his disciples, for there were
many who followed him.
16 And the scribes of the Pharisees, when they saw that he was eating
with sinners and tax collectors, said to his disciples, "Why does
he eat with tax collectors and sinners?"
17 And when Jesus heard it, he said to them, "Those who are well
have no need of a physician, but those who are sick. I came not to
call the righteous, but sinners."

* paralytic [pærəlítik] ⓜ 마비(중풍)환자. ⓗ 마비된. 중풍에 걸린. 무력한.

A Question About Fasting

18 Now John's disciples and the Pharisees were fasting*. And people
came and said to him, "Why do John's disciples and the disciples
of the Pharisees fast, but your disciples do not fast?"
19 And Jesus said to them, "Can the wedding guests fast while
the bridegroom is with them? As long as they have
the bridegroom with them, they cannot fast.
20 The days will come when the bridegroom is taken away from
them, and then they will fast in that day.
21 No one sews a piece of unshrunk cloth on an old garment.
If he does, the patch tears away from it, the new from the old,
and a worse tear is made.
22 And no one puts new wine into old wineskins. If he does,
the wine will burst the skins—and the wine is destroyed, and so
are the skins. But new wine is for fresh wineskins."

Jesus Is Lord of the Sabbath

23 One Sabbath** he was going through the grainfields, and as they
made their way, his disciples began to pluck heads of grain.
24 And the Pharisees were saying to him, "Look, why are they doing
what is not lawful on the Sabbath?"
25 And he said to them, "Have you never read what David did,
when he was in need and was hungry, he and those who were
with him:

* fasting [fǽstiŋ] ⑱ 금식, 단식. ⑲ 금식의, 단식의.

** Sabbath [sǽbəθ] ⑱ 안식일.

26 how he entered the house of God, in the time of Abiathar
the high priest, and ate the bread of the Presence*, which it is not
lawful for any but the priests to eat, and also gave it to those who
were with him?"
27 And he said to them, "The Sabbath was made for man, not man
for the Sabbath.
28 So the Son of Man is lord even of the Sabbath."

* bread of the Presence ⑱ 진설병.

I came not to call the righteous, but sinners. (2:17b)

나는 의인을 부르러 온 것이 아니요 죄인을 부르러 왔노라 하시니라.

하루 한 문장, 생각 쓰기

오늘 본문을 쓰면서 깨달은 지혜, 새롭게 다짐한 점,
떠오른 생각 등을 자유롭게 적어 보세요.

DAY 4

DATE . . .

Mark 3

A Man with a Withered Hand

1 Again he entered the synagogue, and a man was there with
a withered* hand.
2 And they watched Jesus, to see whether he would heal him on
the Sabbath, so that they might accuse him.
3 And he said to the man with the withered hand, "Come here."
4 And he said to them, "Is it lawful on the Sabbath to do good or
to do harm, to save life or to kill?" But they were silent.
5 And he looked around at them with anger, grieved** at their
hardness of heart, and said to the man, "Stretch out your hand."
He stretched it out, and his hand was restored.
6 The Pharisees went out and immediately held counsel with
the Herodians against him, how to destroy him.

A Great Crowd Follows Jesus

7 Jesus withdrew with his disciples to the sea, and a great crowd
followed, from Galilee and Judea

* withered [wíðərd] ⓗ 말라 죽은. 메마른. 여위고 약한.
** grieved [griːvd] ⓗ 슬퍼하는. 슬픈.

8 and Jerusalem and Idumea and from beyond the Jordan and from
around Tyre and Sidon. When the great crowd heard all that he
was doing, they came to him.
9 And he told his disciples to have a boat ready for him because of
the crowd, lest they crush him,
10 for he had healed many, so that all who had diseases pressed
around him to touch him.
11 And whenever the unclean spirits saw him, they fell down before
him and cried out, "You are the Son of God."
12 And he strictly* ordered them not to make him known.

The Twelve Apostles

13 And he went up on the mountain and called to him those whom
he desired, and they came to him.
14 And he appointed twelve (whom he also named apostles) so that
they might be with him and he might send them out to preach
15 and have authority to cast out demons.
16 He appointed the twelve: Simon (to whom he gave the name
Peter);
17 James the son of Zebedee and John the brother of James (to
whom he gave the name Boanerges, that is, Sons of Thunder);
18 Andrew, and Philip, and Bartholomew, and Matthew, and
Thomas, and James the son of Alphaeus, and Thaddaeus, and
Simon the Zealot,

* strictly [stríktli] ㊝ 엄하게. 엄밀히. 절대적으로.

19 and Judas Iscariot, who betrayed* him.

* betray [bitréi] ⓢ 배신하다. 배반하다. 밀고하다.

오늘의 외울 말씀

And said to the man, "Stretch out your hand."
He stretched it out, and his hand was restored. (3:5b)

그 사람에게 이르시되 네 손을 내밀라 하시니
내밀매 그 손이 회복되었더라.

하루 한 문장, 생각 쓰기

오늘 본문을 쓰면서 깨달은 지혜, 새롭게 다짐한 점,
떠오른 생각 등을 자유롭게 적어 보세요.

DATE . . .

Mark 3

20 Then he went home, and the crowd gathered again, so that they
could not even eat.
21 And when his family heard it, they went out to seize him, for they
were saying, "He is out of his mind."

Blasphemy Against the Holy Spirit

22 And the scribes who came down from Jerusalem were saying,
"He is possessed by Beelzebul," and "by the prince of demons he
casts out the demons."
23 And he called them to him and said to them in parables,
"How can Satan cast out Satan?
24 If a kingdom is divided against itself, that kingdom cannot stand.
25 And if a house is divided against itself, that house will not be able
to stand.
26 And if Satan has risen up against himself and is divided,
he cannot stand, but is coming to an end.
27 But no one can enter a strong man's house and plunder his
goods, unless he first binds the strong man. Then indeed he may
plunder* his house.

* plunder [plʌndər] ⓢ 약탈하다. ⓜ 강탈. 약탈.

28 "Truly, I say to you, all sins will be forgiven the children of man,
and whatever blasphemies* they utter,
29 but whoever blasphemes against the Holy Spirit never has
forgiveness, but is guilty of an eternal sin"—
30 for they were saying, "He has an unclean spirit."

Jesus' Mother and Brothers

31 And his mother and his brothers came, and standing outside they
sent to him and called him.
32 And a crowd was sitting around him, and they said to him,
"Your mother and your brothers are outside, seeking you."
33 And he answered them, "Who are my mother and my brothers?"
34 And looking about at those who sat around him, he said,
"Here are my mother and my brothers!
35 For whoever does the will of God, he is my brother and sister and
mother."

* blasphemy [blæsfəmi] ⑱ 신성 모독.

오늘의 외울 말씀

For whoever does the will of God,
he is my brother and sister and mother. (3:35)

누구든지 하나님의 뜻대로 행하는 자가 내 형제요 자매요 어머니이니라.

하루 한 문장, 생각 쓰기

오늘 본문을 쓰면서 깨달은 지혜, 새롭게 다짐한 점,
떠오른 생각 등을 자유롭게 적어 보세요.

DAY 6

DATE . . .

Mark 4

The Parable of the Sower

1 Again he began to teach beside the sea. And a very large crowd
gathered about him, so that he got into a boat and sat in it on
the sea, and the whole crowd was beside the sea on the land.

2 And he was teaching them many things in parables, and in his
teaching he said to them:

3 "Listen! Behold, a sower* went out to sow.

4 And as he sowed, some seed fell along the path, and the birds
came and devoured it.

5 Other seed fell on rocky ground, where it did not have much soil,
and immediately it sprang up, since it had no depth of soil.

6 And when the sun rose, it was scorched, and since it had no root,
it withered away.

7 Other seed fell among thorns, and the thorns grew up and
choked it, and it yielded no grain.

8 And other seeds fell into good soil and produced grain, growing
up and increasing and yielding thirtyfold and sixtyfold and
a hundredfold."

* sower [sóuər] ⑱ 씨 뿌리는 사람.

9 And he said, “He who has ears to hear, let him hear.”

The Purpose of the Parables

10 And when he was alone, those around him with the twelve asked
him about the parables.
11 And he said to them, “To you has been given the secret of
the kingdom of God, but for those outside everything is in
parables,
12 so that “‘they may indeed see but not perceive, and may indeed
hear but not understand, lest they should turn and be forgiven.’”
13 And he said to them, “Do you not understand this parable?
How then will you understand all the parables?
14 The sower sows the word.
15 And these are the ones along the path, where the word is sown:
when they hear, Satan immediately comes and takes away
the word that is sown in them.
16 And these are the ones sown on rocky ground: the ones who,
when they hear the word, immediately receive it with joy.
17 And they have no root in themselves, but endure for a while;
then, when tribulation* or persecution** arises on account of
the word, immediately they fall away.
18 And others are the ones sown among thorns. They are those who
hear the word,

* tribulation [trìbjuléiʃən] ⓜ 고난. 시련.
** persecution [pə̀:rsikjú:ʃən] ⓜ 박해. 핍박.

19 but the cares of the world and the deceitfulness* of riches and
the desires for other things enter in and choke the word,
and it proves unfruitful.
20 But those that were sown on the good soil are the ones who hear
the word and accept it and bear fruit, thirtyfold and sixtyfold and
a hundredfold."

* deceitfulness [disíːtfəlnis] ⓜ 거짓, 속임.

오늘의 외울 말씀

To you has been given the secret of the kingdom of God,
but for those outside everything is in parables,
so that "they may indeed see but not perceive,
and may indeed hear but not understand,
lest they should turn and be forgiven." (4:11-12)

하나님 나라의 비밀을 너희에게는 주었으나
외인에게는 모든 것을 비유로 하나니
이는 그들로 보기는 보아도 알지 못하며
듣기는 들어도 깨닫지 못하게 하여 돌이켜 죄 사함을 얻지 못하게 하려 함이라.

하루 한 문장, 생각 쓰기

오늘 본문을 쓰면서 깨달은 지혜, 새롭게 다짐한 점,
떠오른 생각 등을 자유롭게 적어 보세요.

DAY 7

DATE . . .

Mark 4

A Lamp Under a Basket

21 And he said to them, "Is a lamp brought in to be put under
a basket, or under a bed, and not on a stand?
22 For nothing is hidden except to be made manifest*; nor is
anything secret except to come to light.
23 If anyone has ears to hear, let him hear."
24 And he said to them, "Pay attention to what you hear:
with the measure you use, it will be measured to you,
and still more will be added to you.
25 For to the one who has, more will be given, and from the one
who has not, even what he has will be taken away."

The Parable of the Seed Growing

26 And he said, "The kingdom of God is as if a man should scatter**
seed on the ground.
27 He sleeps and rises night and day, and the seed sprouts and grows;
he knows not how.

* manifest [mænəfèst] ⓢ 나타내다. ⓗ 분명한.

** scatter [skætər] ⓢ 뿌리다. ⓜ 소수(소량).

28 The earth produces by itself, first the blade, then the ear,
then the full grain in the ear.

29 But when the grain is ripe, at once he puts in the sickle*,
because the harvest has come."

The Parable of the Mustard Seed

30 And he said, "With what can we compare the kingdom of God,
or what parable shall we use for it?

31 It is like a grain of mustard seed, which, when sown on
the ground, is the smallest of all the seeds on earth,

32 yet when it is sown it grows up and becomes larger than all
the garden plants and puts out large branches, so that the birds of
the air can make nests in its shade."

33 With many such parables he spoke the word to them, as they were
able to hear it.

34 He did not speak to them without a parable, but privately** to his
own disciples he explained everything.

Jesus Calms a Storm

35 On that day, when evening had come, he said to them,
"Let us go across to the other side."

36 And leaving the crowd, they took him with them in the boat,
just as he was. And other boats were with him.

37 And a great windstorm arose, and the waves were breaking into
the boat, so that the boat was already filling.

* sickle [síkl] ⓜ 낫.

** privately [práivitli] ⓑ 개인적으로, 은밀히.

38 But he was in the stern, asleep on the cushion. And they woke him
and said to him, "Teacher, do you not care that we are perishing*?"
39 And he awoke and rebuked the wind and said to the sea,
"Peace! Be still!" And the wind ceased, and there was a great calm.
40 He said to them, "Why are you so afraid? Have you still no faith?"
41 And they were filled with great fear and said to one another,
"Who then is this, that even the wind and the sea obey him?"

* perishing [périʃiŋ] ⓗ 파괴하는. 고통을 초래하는. 망하는.

오늘의 외울 말씀

And he awoke and rebuked the wind and said to the sea,
"Peace! Be still!" And the wind ceased,
and there was a great calm. (4:39)

예수께서 깨어 바람을 꾸짖으시며 바다더러 이르시되
잠잠하라 고요하라 하시니
바람이 그치고 아주 잔잔하여지더라.

하루 한 문장, 생각 쓰기

오늘 본문을 쓰면서 깨달은 지혜, 새롭게 다짐한 점,
떠오른 생각 등을 자유롭게 적어 보세요.

DAY 8

DATE . . .

Mark 5

Jesus Heals a Man with a Demon

1 They came to the other side of the sea, to the country of
the Gerasenes.

2 And when Jesus had stepped out of the boat, immediately there
met him out of the tombs a man with an unclean spirit.

3 He lived among the tombs. And no one could bind him anymore,
not even with a chain,

4 for he had often been bound with shackles* and chains, but he
wrenched the chains apart, and he broke the shackles in pieces.
No one had the strength to subdue him.

5 Night and day among the tombs and on the mountains he was
always crying out and cutting himself with stones.

6 And when he saw Jesus from afar, he ran and fell down before
him.

7 And crying out with a loud voice, he said, "What have you to
do with me, Jesus, Son of the Most High God? I adjure** you by
God, do not torment me."

* shackles [ʃǽklz] ⓜ 족쇄. 쇠고랑.

** adjure [ədʒúər] ⓢ 명하다. 요구하다. 간청하다.

8 For he was saying to him, "Come out of the man, you unclean
spirit!"
9 And Jesus asked him, "What is your name?"
He replied, "My name is Legion, for we are many."
10 And he begged* him earnestly not to send them out of the country.
11 Now a great herd of pigs was feeding there on the hillside,
12 and they begged him, saying, "Send us to the pigs; let us enter
them."
13 So he gave them permission. And the unclean spirits came
out and entered the pigs; and the herd, numbering about two
thousand, rushed down the steep bank into the sea and drowned
in the sea.
14 The herdsmen fled and told it in the city and in the country.
And people came to see what it was that had happened.
15 And they came to Jesus and saw the demon-possessed man,
the one who had had the legion, sitting there, clothed and in his
right mind, and they were afraid.
16 And those who had seen it described to them what had happened
to the demon-possessed man and to the pigs.
17 And they began to beg Jesus to depart from their region.
18 As he was getting into the boat, the man who had been possessed**
with demons begged him that he might be with him.

* beg [beg] ⑧ 간청하다. 구걸하다.
** possessed [pəzést] ⑱ 홀린.

19 And he did not permit him but said to him, "Go home to your
friends and tell them how much the Lord has done for you,
and how he has had mercy on you."
20 And he went away and began to proclaim in the Decapolis how
much Jesus had done for him, and everyone marveled.

오늘의 외울 말씀

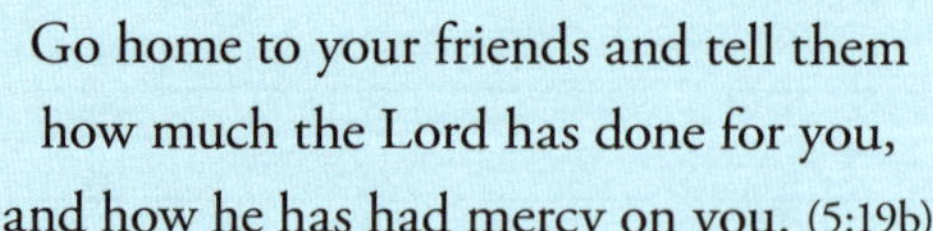

Go home to your friends and tell them
how much the Lord has done for you,
and how he has had mercy on you. (5:19b)

집으로 돌아가 주께서 네게 어떻게 큰 일을 행하사
너를 불쌍히 여기신 것을 네 가족에게 알리라.

하루 한 문장, 생각 쓰기

오늘 본문을 쓰면서 깨달은 지혜, 새롭게 다짐한 점,
떠오른 생각 등을 자유롭게 적어 보세요.

DAY 9

Mark 5

DATE . . .

Jesus Heals a Woman and Jairus's Daughter

21 And when Jesus had crossed again in the boat to the other side,
a great crowd gathered about him, and he was beside the sea.
22 Then came one of the rulers of the synagogue, Jairus by name,
and seeing him, he fell at his feet
23 and implored him earnestly*, saying, "My little daughter is at
the point of death. Come and lay your hands on her, so that she
may be made well and live."
24 And he went with him. And a great crowd followed him and
thronged** about him.
25 And there was a woman who had had a discharge of blood for
twelve years,
26 and who had suffered much under many physicians, and had
spent all that she had, and was no better but rather grew worse.
27 She had heard the reports about Jesus and came up behind him
in the crowd and touched his garment.
28 For she said, "If I touch even his garments, I will be made well."

* earnestly [ə́ːrnistli] ㊙ 진지하게. 진정으로.

** throng [θrɔːŋ] ㊔ 군중. 인파. ㊓ 모여들다.

29 And immediately the flow of blood dried up, and she felt in her body that she was healed of her disease.

30 And Jesus, perceiving in himself that power had gone out from him, immediately turned about in the crowd and said, "Who touched my garments?"

31 And his disciples said to him, "You see the crowd pressing around you, and yet you say, 'Who touched me?'"

32 And he looked around to see who had done it.

33 But the woman, knowing what had happened to her, came in fear and trembling* and fell down before him and told him the whole truth.

34 And he said to her, "Daughter, your faith has made you well; go in peace, and be healed of your disease."

35 While he was still speaking, there came from the ruler's house some who said, "Your daughter is dead. Why trouble the Teacher any further?"

36 But overhearing what they said, Jesus said to the ruler of the synagogue, "Do not fear, only believe."

37 And he allowed no one to follow him except Peter and James and John the brother of James.

38 They came to the house of the ruler of the synagogue, and Jesus saw a commotion**, people weeping and wailing loudly.

39 And when he had entered, he said to them, "Why are you making a commotion and weeping? The child is not dead but sleeping."

* trembling [trémbliŋ] ㉺ 떨림. 전율. ㉿ 떨리는. 전율하는.

** commotion [kəmóuʃən] ㉺ 소란. 소동.

40 And they laughed at him. But he put them all outside and took
the child's father and mother and those who were with him and
went in where the child was.
41 Taking her by the hand he said to her, "Talitha cumi," which
means, "Little girl, I say to you, arise."
42 And immediately the girl got up and began walking (for she was
twelve years of age), and they were immediately overcome with
amazement.
43 And he strictly charged them that no one should know this,
and told them to give her something to eat.

오늘의 외울 말씀

And he said to her,
"Daughter, your faith has made you well; go in peace,
and be healed of your disease." (5:34)

예수께서 이르시되 딸아 네 믿음이 너를 구원하였으니 평안히 가라
네 병에서 놓여 건강할지어다.

하루 한 문장, 생각 쓰기

오늘 본문을 쓰면서 깨달은 지혜, 새롭게 다짐한 점,
떠오른 생각 등을 자유롭게 적어 보세요.

DAY 10

DATE . . .

Mark 6

Jesus Rejected at Nazareth

1 He went away from there and came to his hometown, and his
disciples followed him.

2 And on the Sabbath he began to teach in the synagogue,
and many who heard him were astonished, saying,
"Where did this man get these things? What is the wisdom given
to him? How are such mighty works done by his hands?

3 Is not this the carpenter, the son of Mary and brother of James
and Joses and Judas and Simon? And are not his sisters here with
us?" And they took offense at him.

4 And Jesus said to them, "A prophet* is not without honor,
except in his hometown and among his relatives and in his own
household."

5 And he could do no mighty work there, except that he laid his
hands on a few sick people and healed them.

6 And he marveled because of their unbelief. And he went about
among the villages teaching.

* prophet [prάfit] ⑲ 선지자.

Jesus Sends Out the Twelve Apostles

7 And he called the twelve and began to send them out two by two,
and gave them authority over the unclean spirits.

8 He charged them to take nothing for their journey except a staff—
no bread, no bag, no money in their belts—

9 but to wear sandals and not put on two tunics.

10 And he said to them, "Whenever you enter a house, stay there
until you depart from there.

11 And if any place will not receive you and they will not listen to
you, when you leave, shake off the dust that is on your feet as
a testimony* against them."

12 So they went out and proclaimed that people should repent.

13 And they cast out many demons and anointed with oil many who
were sick and healed them.

The Death of John the Baptist

14 King Herod heard of it, for Jesus' name had become known.
Some said, "John the Baptist has been raised from the dead.
That is why these miraculous powers are at work in him."

15 But others said, "He is Elijah." And others said, "He is a prophet,
like one of the prophets of old."

16 But when Herod heard of it, he said, "John, whom I beheaded**,
has been raised."

* testimony [téstəmòuni] ⓜ 증거. 증언.

** behead [bihéd] ⓢ 목을 베다. 참수하다.

17 For it was Herod who had sent and seized John and bound him
in prison for the sake of Herodias, his brother Philip's wife,
because he had married her.

18 For John had been saying to Herod, "It is not lawful for you to
have your brother's wife."

19 And Herodias had a grudge* against him and wanted to put him
to death. But she could not,

20 for Herod feared John, knowing that he was a righteous and holy
man, and he kept him safe. When he heard him, he was greatly
perplexed, and yet he heard him gladly.

21 But an opportunity came when Herod on his birthday gave
a banquet for his nobles and military commanders and
the leading men of Galilee.

22 For when Herodias's daughter came in and danced, she pleased
Herod and his guests. And the king said to the girl,
"Ask me for whatever you wish, and I will give it to you."

23 And he vowed to her, "Whatever you ask me, I will give you,
up to half of my kingdom."

24 And she went out and said to her mother, "For what should I
ask?" And she said, "The head of John the Baptist."

25 And she came in immediately with haste to the king and asked,
saying, "I want you to give me at once the head of John
the Baptist on a platter."

26 And the king was exceedingly** sorry, but because of his oaths and
his guests he did not want to break his word to her.

* grudge [grʌdʒ] ㉮ 원한, 악의. ㉯ 나쁘게 생각하다.

** exceedingly [iksíːdiŋli] ㉯ 몹시, 과하게, 극도로.

27 And immediately the king sent an executioner* with orders to
bring John's head. He went and beheaded him in the prison
28 and brought his head on a platter and gave it to the girl,
and the girl gave it to her mother.
29 When his disciples heard of it, they came and took his body and
laid it in a tomb.

* executioner [èksikjúːʃənər] ⑲ 사형 집행인.

오늘의 외울 말씀

And Jesus said to them, "A prophet is not without honor, except in his hometown and among his relatives and in his own household." (6:4)

예수께서 그들에게 이르시되 선지자가 자기 고향과 자기 친척과 자기 집 외에서는 존경을 받지 못함이 없느니라 하시며.

하루 한 문장, 생각 쓰기

오늘 본문을 쓰면서 깨달은 지혜, 새롭게 다짐한 점,
떠오른 생각 등을 자유롭게 적어 보세요.

DAY 11

DATE . . .

Mark 6

Jesus Feeds the Five Thousand

30 The apostles* returned to Jesus and told him all that they had
done and taught.

31 And he said to them, "Come away by yourselves to a desolate
place and rest a while." For many were coming and going,
and they had no leisure even to eat.

32 And they went away in the boat to a desolate place by themselves.

33 Now many saw them going and recognized them, and they ran
there on foot from all the towns and got there ahead of them.

34 When he went ashore he saw a great crowd, and he had
compassion on them, because they were like sheep without
a shepherd. And he began to teach them many things.

35 And when it grew late, his disciples came to him and said,
"This is a desolate place, and the hour is now late.

36 Send them away to go into the surrounding countryside and
villages and buy themselves something to eat."

* apostle [əpɑ́sl] ⓜ 사도, 주창자.

37 But he answered them, "You give them something to eat."
And they said to him, "Shall we go and buy two hundred denarii
worth of bread and give it to them to eat?"
38 And he said to them, "How many loaves do you have? Go and
see." And when they had found out, they said, "Five, and two
fish."
39 Then he commanded them all to sit down in groups on the green
grass.
40 So they sat down in groups, by hundreds and by fifties.
41 And taking the five loaves and the two fish, he looked up to
heaven and said a blessing and broke the loaves and gave them to
the disciples to set before the people. And he divided the two fish
among them all.
42 And they all ate and were satisfied.
43 And they took up twelve baskets full of broken pieces and of
the fish.
44 And those who ate the loaves were five thousand men.

Jesus Walks on the Water

45 Immediately he made his disciples get into the boat and go before
him to the other side, to Bethsaida, while he dismissed the crowd.
46 And after he had taken leave of them, he went up on
the mountain to pray.
47 And when evening came, the boat was out on the sea, and he was
alone on the land.

48 And he saw that they were making headway painfully,
for the wind was against them. And about the fourth watch of
the night he came to them, walking on the sea. He meant to pass
by them,
49 but when they saw him walking on the sea they thought it was
a ghost, and cried out,
50 for they all saw him and were terrified. But immediately he spoke
to them and said, "Take heart; it is I. Do not be afraid."
51 And he got into the boat with them, and the wind ceased*.
And they were utterly astounded**,
52 for they did not understand about the loaves, but their hearts
were hardened***.

Jesus Heals the Sick in Gennesaret

53 When they had crossed over, they came to land at Gennesaret and
moored to the shore.
54 And when they got out of the boat, the people immediately
recognized him
55 and ran about the whole region and began to bring the sick
people on their beds to wherever they heard he was.
56 And wherever he came, in villages, cities, or countryside, they laid
the sick in the marketplaces and implored him that they might
touch even the fringe of his garment. And as many as touched it
were made well.

* cease [siːs] ⓢ 그치다. 중단하다.

** astounded [əstáundid] ⓗ 아연실색한. 몹시 놀란.

*** hardened [hɑ́ːrdnd] ⓗ 굳어진. 무정한. 완고한.

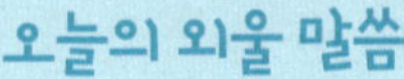

When he went ashore he saw a great crowd,
and he had compassion on them,
because they were like sheep without a shepherd.
And he began to teach them many things. (6:34)

예수께서 나오사 큰 무리를 보시고
그 목자 없는 양 같음으로 인하여 불쌍히 여기사
이에 여러 가지로 가르치시더라.

하루 한 문장, 생각 쓰기

오늘 본문을 쓰면서 깨달은 지혜, 새롭게 다짐한 점,
떠오른 생각 등을 자유롭게 적어 보세요.

DAY 12

DATE . . .

Mark 7

Traditions and Commandments

1 Now when the Pharisees gathered to him, with some of the scribes
who had come from Jerusalem,
2 they saw that some of his disciples ate with hands that were
defiled, that is, unwashed.
3 (For the Pharisees and all the Jews do not eat unless they wash
their hands properly, holding to the tradition of the elders,
4 and when they come from the marketplace, they do not eat
unless they wash. And there are many other traditions that they
observe, such as the washing of cups and pots and copper vessels
and dining couches.)
5 And the Pharisees and the scribes asked him, "Why do your
disciples not walk according to the tradition of the elders, but eat
with defiled hands?"
6 And he said to them, "Well did Isaiah prophesy of you hypocrites,
as it is written, "'This people honors me with their lips, but their
heart is far from me;
7 in vain do they worship me,
teaching as doctrines the commandments of men.'

8 You leave the commandment* of God and hold to the tradition of
men."
9 And he said to them, "You have a fine way of rejecting
the commandment of God in order to establish your tradition!
10 For Moses said, 'Honor your father and your mother'; and,
'Whoever reviles father or mother must surely die.'
11 But you say, 'If a man tells his father or his mother, "Whatever
you would have gained from me is Corban"' (that is, given to
God)—
12 then you no longer permit him to do anything for his father or
mother,
13 thus making void the word of God by your tradition that you
have handed down. And many such things you do."

What Defiles a Person

14 And he called the people to him again and said to them,
"Hear me, all of you, and understand:
15 There is nothing outside a person that by going into him can
defile** him, but the things that come out of a person are what
defile him."
17 And when he had entered the house and left the people,
his disciples asked him about the parable.
18 And he said to them, "Then are you also without understanding?
Do you not see that whatever goes into a person from outside
cannot defile him,

* commandment [kəmǽndmənt] ⓜ 계명.
** defile [difáil] ⓢ 더럽히다.

19 since it enters not his heart but his stomach, and is expelled*?"
(Thus he declared all foods clean.)
20 And he said, "What comes out of a person is what defiles him.
21 For from within, out of the heart of man, come evil thoughts,
sexual immorality, theft, murder, adultery,
22 coveting, wickedness, deceit, sensuality, envy, slander, pride,
foolishness.
23 All these evil things come from within, and they defile a person."

* expel [ikspél] ⑧ 배출하다. 방출하다. 쫓아내다.

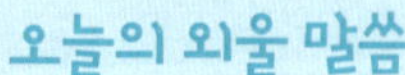

And he said, "What comes out of a person is what defiles him." (7:20)

또 이르시되 사람에게서 나오는 그것이 사람을 더럽게 하느니라.

하루 한 문장, 생각 쓰기

오늘 본문을 쓰면서 깨달은 지혜, 새롭게 다짐한 점,
떠오른 생각 등을 자유롭게 적어 보세요.

DAY 13

DATE . . .

Mark 7

The Syrophoenician Woman's Faith

24 And from there he arose and went away to the region of Tyre and
Sidon. And he entered a house and did not want anyone to know,
yet he could not be hidden.

25 But immediately a woman whose little daughter had an unclean
spirit heard of him and came and fell down at his feet.

26 Now the woman was a Gentile, a Syrophoenician by birth.
And she begged him to cast the demon out of her daughter.

27 And he said to her, "Let the children be fed first, for it is not right
to take the children's bread and throw it to the dogs."

28 But she answered him, "Yes, Lord; yet even the dogs under
the table eat the children's crumbs*."

29 And he said to her, "For this statement you may go your way;
the demon has left your daughter."

30 And she went home and found the child lying in bed and
the demon gone.

* crumb [krʌm] ⑱ 부스러기. 빵가루.

Jesus Heals a Deaf Man

31 Then he returned from the region of Tyre and went through Sidon to the Sea of Galilee, in the region of the Decapolis.

32 And they brought to him a man who was deaf and had a speech impediment, and they begged him to lay his hand on him.

33 And taking him aside from the crowd privately, he put his fingers into his ears, and after spitting touched his tongue.

34 And looking up to heaven, he sighed* and said to him, "Ephphatha," that is, "Be opened."

35 And his ears were opened, his tongue was released, and he spoke plainly.

36 And Jesus charged them to tell no one. But the more he charged them, the more zealously** they proclaimed it.

37 And they were astonished beyond measure, saying, "He has done all things well. He even makes the deaf hear and the mute speak."

* sigh [sai] ⓢ 탄식하다. 한숨을 쉬다. ⓜ 한숨.

** zealously [zéləsli] ⓑ 열심히. 열광적으로.

오늘의 외울 말씀

And looking up to heaven, he sighed and said to him, "Ephphatha," that is, "Be opened." And his ears were opened, his tongue was released, and he spoke plainly. (7:34-35)

하늘을 우러러 탄식하시며 그에게 이르시되
에바다 하시니 이는 열리라는 뜻이라
그의 귀가 열리고 혀가 맺힌 것이 곧 풀려 말이 분명하여졌더라.

하루 한 문장, 생각 쓰기

오늘 본문을 쓰면서 깨달은 지혜, 새롭게 다짐한 점,
떠오른 생각 등을 자유롭게 적어 보세요.

DAY 14

DATE . . .

Mark 8

Jesus Feeds the Four Thousand

1 In those days, when again a great crowd had gathered, and they
had nothing to eat, he called his disciples to him and said to them,

2 "I have compassion on the crowd, because they have been with
me now three days and have nothing to eat.

3 And if I send them away hungry to their homes, they will faint
on the way. And some of them have come from far away."

4 And his disciples answered him, "How can one feed these people
with bread here in this desolate place?"

5 And he asked them, "How many loaves do you have?" They said,
"Seven."

6 And he directed the crowd to sit down on the ground. And he
took the seven loaves, and having given thanks, he broke them
and gave them to his disciples to set before the people; and they
set them before the crowd.

7 And they had a few small fish. And having blessed them, he said
that these also should be set before them.

8 And they ate and were satisfied. And they took up the broken
pieces left over, seven baskets full.

9 And there were about four thousand people. And he sent them away.

10 And immediately he got into the boat with his disciples and went to the district of Dalmanutha.

The Pharisees Demand a Sign

11 The Pharisees* came and began to argue with him, seeking from him a sign from heaven to test him.

12 And he sighed deeply in his spirit and said,
"Why does this generation seek a sign? Truly, I say to you, no sign will be given to this generation."

13 And he left them, got into the boat again, and went to the other side.

The Leaven of the Pharisees and Herod

14 Now they had forgotten to bring bread, and they had only one loaf with them in the boat.

15 And he cautioned them, saying, "Watch out; beware of the leaven of the Pharisees and the leaven of Herod."

16 And they began discussing with one another the fact that they had no bread.

17 And Jesus, aware of this, said to them, "Why are you discussing the fact that you have no bread? Do you not yet perceive or understand? Are your hearts hardened?

* Pharisee [fǽrisìː] ⓜ 바리새인.

18 Having eyes do you not see, and having ears do you not hear? And do you not remember?

19 When I broke the five loaves for the five thousand, how many baskets full of broken pieces did you take up?" They said to him, "Twelve."

20 "And the seven for the four thousand, how many baskets full of broken pieces did you take up?" And they said to him, "Seven."

21 And he said to them, "Do you not yet understand?"

오늘의 외울 말씀

And he cautioned them, saying,
"Watch out; beware of the leaven of the Pharisees
and the leaven of Herod." (8:15)

예수께서 경고하여 이르시되
삼가 바리새인들의 누룩과 헤롯의 누룩을 주의하라 하시니.

하루 한 문장, 생각 쓰기

오늘 본문을 쓰면서 깨달은 지혜, 새롭게 다짐한 점,
떠오른 생각 등을 자유롭게 적어 보세요.

DAY 15

DATE . . .

Mark 8

Jesus Heals a Blind Man at Bethsaida

22 And they came to Bethsaida. And some people brought to him
a blind man and begged him to touch him.

23 And he took the blind man by the hand and led him out of
the village, and when he had spit on his eyes and laid his hands
on him, he asked him, "Do you see anything?"

24 And he looked up and said, "I see people, but they look like trees,
walking."

25 Then Jesus laid his hands on* his eyes again; and he opened his
eyes, his sight was restored**, and he saw everything clearly.

26 And he sent him to his home, saying, "Do not even enter
the village."

Peter Confesses Jesus as the Christ

27 And Jesus went on with his disciples to the villages of Caesarea
Philippi. And on the way he asked his disciples, "Who do people
say that I am?"

* laying one's hands on ⓜ 안수.

** restore [ristɔ́:r] ⓢ 회복하다, 되찾다.

28 And they told him, "John the Baptist; and others say, Elijah;
and others, one of the prophets."

29 And he asked them, "But who do you say that I am?" Peter
answered him, "You are the Christ."

30 And he strictly charged them to tell no one about him.

Jesus Foretells His Death and Resurrection

31 And he began to teach them that the Son of Man must suffer
many things and be rejected by the elders and the chief priests
and the scribes and be killed, and after three days rise again.

32 And he said this plainly. And Peter took him aside and began to
rebuke* him.

33 But turning and seeing his disciples, he rebuked Peter and said,
"Get behind me, Satan! For you are not setting your mind on
the things of God, but on the things of man."

34 And calling the crowd to him with his disciples, he said to them,
"If anyone would come after me, let him deny himself and take
up his cross and follow me.

35 For whoever would save his life will lose it, but whoever loses his
life for my sake and the gospel's will save it.

36 For what does it profit a man to gain the whole world and forfeit**
his soul?

37 For what can a man give in return for his soul?

* rebuke [ribjúːk] ⓢ 질책하다. ⓜ 심한 비난.

** forfeit [fɔ́ːrfit] ⓢ 몰수당하다. ⓜ 몰수. 박탈. ⓗ 몰수된. 박탈당한.

38 For whoever is ashamed of me and of my words in this adulterous*
and sinful generation, of him will the Son of Man also be ashamed
when he comes in the glory of his Father with the holy angels."

* adulterous [ədʌltərəs] ⓗ 부정한. 불륜의. 불의의.

오늘의 외울 말씀

If anyone would come after me,
let him deny himself and take up his cross and follow me. (8:34b)

누구든지 나를 따라오려거든
자기를 부인하고 자기 십자가를 지고 나를 따를 것이니라.

하루 한 문장, 생각 쓰기

오늘 본문을 쓰면서 깨달은 지혜, 새롭게 다짐한 점,
떠오른 생각 등을 자유롭게 적어 보세요.

DATE . . .

Mark 9

1 And he said to them, "Truly, I say to you, there are some standing
here who will not taste death until they see the kingdom of God
after it has come with power."

The Transfiguration

2 And after six days Jesus took with him Peter and James and John,
and led them up a high mountain by themselves. And he was
transfigured before them,
3 and his clothes became radiant, intensely* white, as no one on
earth could bleach them.
4 And there appeared to them Elijah with Moses, and they were
talking with Jesus.
5 And Peter said to Jesus, "Rabbi, it is good that we are here.
Let us make three tents, one for you and one for Moses and one
for Elijah."
6 For he did not know what to say, for they were terrified.
7 And a cloud overshadowed them, and a voice came out of
the cloud, "This is my beloved Son; listen to him."

* intensely [inténsli] ㊫ 강렬하게. 격렬히. 열심히.

8 And suddenly, looking around, they no longer saw anyone with
them but Jesus only.
9 And as they were coming down the mountain, he charged them
to tell no one what they had seen, until the Son of Man had risen
from the dead.
10 So they kept the matter to themselves, questioning what this
rising from the dead might mean.
11 And they asked him, "Why do the scribes say that first Elijah
must come?"
12 And he said to them, "Elijah does come first to restore all things.
And how is it written of the Son of Man that he should suffer
many things and be treated with contempt*?
13 But I tell you that Elijah has come, and they did to him whatever
they pleased, as it is written of him."

Jesus Heals a Boy with an Unclean Spirit

14 And when they came to the disciples, they saw a great crowd
around them, and scribes arguing with them.
15 And immediately all the crowd, when they saw him, were greatly
amazed and ran up to him and greeted him.
16 And he asked them, "What are you arguing about with them?"
17 And someone from the crowd answered him, "Teacher, I brought
my son to you, for he has a spirit that makes him mute**.

* contempt [kəntémpt] ⓜ 멸시, 경멸, 무시.

** mute [mju:t] ⓗ 말 못하는. ⓜ (장애로 인한)벙어리.

18 And whenever it seizes him, it throws him down, and he foams
and grinds his teeth and becomes rigid.
So I asked your disciples to cast it out, and they were not able."
19 And he answered them, "O faithless generation, how long am I to
be with you? How long am I to bear with you? Bring him to me."
20 And they brought the boy to him. And when the spirit saw him,
immediately it convulsed* the boy, and he fell on the ground and
rolled about, foaming at the mouth.
21 And Jesus asked his father, "How long has this been happening to
him?" And he said, "From childhood.
22 And it has often cast him into fire and into water, to destroy him.
But if you can do anything, have compassion on us and help us."
23 And Jesus said to him, "'If you can'! All things are possible for one
who believes."
24 Immediately the father of the child cried out and said, "I believe;
help my unbelief!"
25 And when Jesus saw that a crowd came running together,
he rebuked the unclean spirit, saying to it, "You mute and deaf
spirit, I command you, come out of him and never enter him
again."
26 And after crying out and convulsing him terribly, it came out, and
the boy was like a corpse**, so that most of them said, "He is dead."
27 But Jesus took him by the hand and lifted him up, and he arose.

* convulse [kənvʌls] ⓢ 경련을 일으키게 하다. 경련하다.
** corpse [kɔːrps] ⓜ 시체. 송장. 효력을 잃은 것.

28 And when he had entered the house, his disciples asked him privately, "Why could we not cast it out?"

29 And he said to them, "This kind cannot be driven out by anything but prayer."

오늘의 외울 말씀

And Jesus said to him,
"'If you can'! All things are possible for one who believes." (9:23)

예수께서 이르시되 할 수 있거든이 무슨 말이냐
믿는 자에게는 능히 하지 못할 일이 없느니라 하시니.

하루 한 문장, 생각 쓰기

오늘 본문을 쓰면서 깨달은 지혜, 새롭게 다짐한 점,
떠오른 생각 등을 자유롭게 적어 보세요.

DAY 17

DATE . . .

Mark 9

Jesus Again Foretells Death, Resurrection

30 They went on from there and passed through Galilee. And he did
not want anyone to know,
31 for he was teaching his disciples, saying to them, "The Son of
Man is going to be delivered into the hands of men, and they will
kill him. And when he is killed, after three days he will rise."
32 But they did not understand the saying, and were afraid to ask
him.

Who Is the Greatest?

33 And they came to Capernaum. And when he was in the house he
asked them, "What were you discussing on the way?"
34 But they kept silent, for on the way they had argued with one
another about who was the greatest.
35 And he sat down and called the twelve. And he said to them,
"If anyone would be first, he must be last of all and servant of all."
36 And he took a child and put him in the midst of them,
and taking him in his arms, he said to them,

37 "Whoever receives one such child in my name receives me,
and whoever receives me, receives not me but him who sent me."

Anyone Not Against Us Is for Us

38 John said to him, "Teacher, we saw someone casting out demons
in your name, and we tried to stop him, because he was not
following us."
39 But Jesus said, "Do not stop him, for no one who does a mighty
work in my name will be able soon afterward to speak evil of me.
40 For the one who is not against us is for us.
41 For truly, I say to you, whoever gives you a cup of water to drink
because you belong to Christ will by no means lose his reward.

Temptations to Sin

42 "Whoever causes one of these little ones who believe in me to sin,
it would be better for him if a great millstone were hung around
his neck and he were thrown into the sea.
43 And if your hand causes you to sin, cut it off. It is better for you
to enter life crippled* than with two hands to go to hell,
to the unquenchable fire.
45 And if your foot causes you to sin, cut it off. It is better for you to
enter life lame than with two feet to be thrown into hell.
47 And if your eye causes you to sin, tear it out. It is better for you
to enter the kingdom of God with one eye than with two eyes to
be thrown into hell,

* crippled [krípld] ⓗ 불구의. 무능력한.

48 'where their worm does not die and the fire is not quenched*.'

49 For everyone will be salted with fire.

50 Salt is good, but if the salt has lost its saltiness, how will you make
it salty again? Have salt in yourselves, and be at peace with one
another."

* quench [kwentʃ] 동 (불, 불꽃, 등불 등을) 끄다, 잃게 하다.

오늘의 외울 말씀

Whoever receives one such child in my name receives me,
and whoever receives me, receives not me
but him who sent me. (9:37)

누구든지 내 이름으로 이런 어린 아이 하나를 영접하면 곧 나를 영접함이요
누구든지 나를 영접하면 나를 영접함이 아니요
나를 보내신 이를 영접함이니라.

하루 한 문장, 생각 쓰기

오늘 본문을 쓰면서 깨달은 지혜, 새롭게 다짐한 점,
떠오른 생각 등을 자유롭게 적어 보세요.

DAY 18

DATE . . .

Mark 10

Teaching About Divorce

1 And he left there and went to the region of Judea and beyond
the Jordan, and crowds gathered to him again. And again, as was
his custom, he taught them.

2 And Pharisees came up and in order to test him asked, “Is it
lawful for a man to divorce his wife?”

3 He answered them, “What did Moses command you?”

4 They said, “Moses allowed a man to write a certificate of divorce
and to send her away.”

5 And Jesus said to them, “Because of your hardness of heart he
wrote you this commandment.

6 But from the beginning of creation, ‘God made them male and
female.’

7 ‘Therefore a man shall leave his father and mother and hold fast
to his wife,

8 and the two shall become one flesh.’ So they are no longer two
but one flesh.

9 What therefore God has joined together, let not man separate.”

10 And in the house the disciples asked him again about this matter.
11 And he said to them, "Whoever divorces his wife and marries
another commits adultery against her,
12 and if she divorces her husband and marries another, she commits
adultery."

Let the Children Come to Me

13 And they were bringing children to him that he might touch
them, and the disciples rebuked them.
14 But when Jesus saw it, he was indignant* and said to them,
"Let the children come to me; do not hinder** them, for to such
belongs the kingdom of God.
15 Truly, I say to you, whoever does not receive the kingdom of God
like a child shall not enter it."
16 And he took them in his arms and blessed them, laying his hands
on them.

The Rich Young Man

17 And as he was setting out on his journey, a man ran up and knelt
before him and asked him, "Good Teacher, what must I do to
inherit*** eternal life?"
18 And Jesus said to him, "Why do you call me good? No one is
good except God alone.

* indignant [indígnənt] 형 분개한. 화난.
** hinder [híndər] 동 방해하다. 저해하다. 막다.
*** inherit [inhérit] 동 상속받다. 물려받다.

19 You know the commandments: 'Do not murder, Do not commit
adultery, Do not steal, Do not bear false witness, Do not defraud*,
Honor your father and mother.'"

20 And he said to him, "Teacher, all these I have kept from my
youth."

21 And Jesus, looking at him, loved him, and said to him, "You lack
one thing: go, sell all that you have and give to the poor, and you
will have treasure in heaven; and come, follow me."

22 Disheartened by the saying, he went away sorrowful, for he had
great possessions.

23 And Jesus looked around and said to his disciples, "How difficult
it will be for those who have wealth to enter the kingdom of God!"

24 And the disciples were amazed at his words. But Jesus said to them
again, "Children, how difficult it is to enter the kingdom of God!

25 It is easier for a camel to go through the eye of a needle than for
a rich person to enter the kingdom of God."

26 And they were exceedingly astonished, and said to him, "Then
who can be saved?"

27 Jesus looked at them and said, "With man it is impossible,
but not with God. For all things are possible with God."

28 Peter began to say to him, "See, we have left everything and
followed you."

29 Jesus said, "Truly, I say to you, there is no one who has left house
or brothers or sisters or mother or father or children or lands,
for my sake and for the gospel,

* defraud [difrɔ́:d] 동 사취하다. 속여 빼앗다. 횡령하다.

30 who will not receive a hundredfold now in this time, houses and
brothers and sisters and mothers and children and lands,
with persecutions, and in the age to come eternal life.
31 But many who are first will be last, and the last first."

오늘의 외울 말씀

Let the children come to me; do not hinder them,
for to such belongs the kingdom of God. (10:14b)

어린 아이들이 내게 오는 것을 용납하고 금하지 말라
하나님의 나라가 이런 자의 것이니라.

하루 한 문장, 생각 쓰기

오늘 본문을 쓰면서 깨달은 지혜, 새롭게 다짐한 점,
떠오른 생각 등을 자유롭게 적어 보세요.

DAY 19

DATE . . .

Mark 10

Jesus Foretells His Death a Third Time

32 And they were on the road, going up to Jerusalem, and Jesus was
walking ahead of them. And they were amazed, and those who
followed were afraid. And taking the twelve again, he began to
tell them what was to happen to him,
33 saying, "See, we are going up to Jerusalem, and the Son of Man
will be delivered over to the chief priests and the scribes, and they will
condemn him to death and deliver him over to the Gentiles.
34 And they will mock* him and spit on him, and flog him and kill
him. And after three days he will rise."

The Request of James and John

35 And James and John, the sons of Zebedee, came up to him and
said to him, "Teacher, we want you to do for us whatever we ask
of you."
36 And he said to them, "What do you want me to do for you?"
37 And they said to him, "Grant us to sit, one at your right hand
and one at your left, in your glory."

* mock [mak] ⓢ 조롱하다. 업신여기다. ⓜ 조롱. 조소. ⓗ 가짜의. 거짓의.

38 Jesus said to them, "You do not know what you are asking.
Are you able to drink the cup that I drink, or to be baptized with
the baptism* with which I am baptized?"
39 And they said to him, "We are able." And Jesus said to them,
"The cup that I drink you will drink, and with the baptism with
which I am baptized, you will be baptized,
40 but to sit at my right hand or at my left is not mine to grant,
but it is for those for whom it has been prepared."
41 And when the ten heard it, they began to be indignant at James
and John.
42 And Jesus called them to him and said to them, "You know that
those who are considered rulers of the Gentiles lord it over them,
and their great ones exercise authority over them.
43 But it shall not be so among you. But whoever would be great
among you must be your servant,
44 and whoever would be first among you must be slave of all.
45 For even the Son of Man came not to be served but to serve,
and to give his life as a ransom** for many."

Jesus Heals Blind Bartimaeus

46 And they came to Jericho. And as he was leaving Jericho with his
disciples and a great crowd, Bartimaeus, a blind beggar, the son of
Timaeus, was sitting by the roadside.
47 And when he heard that it was Jesus of Nazareth, he began to cry
out and say, "Jesus, Son of David, have mercy on me!"

* baptism [bǽptizm] ⓜ 세례.

** ransom [rǽnsəm] ⓜ 몸값. 속전. 배상금. ⓢ 몸값을 지불하다. 구해내다.

48 And many rebuked him, telling him to be silent. But he cried out
all the more, "Son of David, have mercy on me!"
49 And Jesus stopped and said, "Call him." And they called the blind
man, saying to him, "Take heart. Get up; he is calling you."
50 And throwing off his cloak*, he sprang up and came to Jesus.
51 And Jesus said to him, "What do you want me to do for you?"
And the blind man said to him, "Rabbi, let me recover my sight."
52 And Jesus said to him, "Go your way; your faith has made you
well." And immediately he recovered his sight and followed him
on the way.

* cloak [klouk] ⓜ 망토. 소매 없는 외투. ⓢ ~에 가리다.

오늘의 외울 말씀

For even the Son of Man came not to be served but to serve,
and to give his life as a ransom for many. (10:45)

인자가 온 것은 섬김을 받으려 함이 아니라 도리어 섬기려 하고
자기 목숨을 많은 사람의 대속물로 주려 함이니라.

하루 한 문장, 생각 쓰기

오늘 본문을 쓰면서 깨달은 지혜, 새롭게 다짐한 점,
떠오른 생각 등을 자유롭게 적어 보세요.

DAY 20

DATE . . .

Mark 11

The Triumphal Entry

1 Now when they drew near to Jerusalem, to Bethphage and
Bethany, at the Mount of Olives, Jesus sent two of his disciples

2 and said to them, "Go into the village in front of you,
and immediately as you enter it you will find a colt tied, on which
no one has ever sat. Untie it and bring it.

3 If anyone says to you, 'Why are you doing this?' say,
'The Lord has need of it and will send it back here immediately.'"

4 And they went away and found a colt* tied at a door outside in
the street, and they untied it.

5 And some of those standing there said to them, "What are you
doing, untying the colt?"

6 And they told them what Jesus had said, and they let them go.

7 And they brought the colt to Jesus and threw their cloaks on it,
and he sat on it.

8 And many spread their cloaks on the road, and others spread leafy
branches that they had cut from the fields.

* colt [koult] ⓜ 수망아지.

9 And those who went before and those who followed were
shouting, "Hosanna! Blessed is he who comes in the name of
the Lord!
10 Blessed is the coming kingdom of our father David! Hosanna in
the highest!"
11 And he entered Jerusalem and went into the temple*. And when
he had looked around at everything, as it was already late, he went
out to Bethany with the twelve.

Jesus Curses the Fig Tree

12 On the following day, when they came from Bethany, he was
hungry.
13 And seeing in the distance a fig tree in leaf, he went to see if he
could find anything on it. When he came to it, he found nothing
but leaves, for it was not the season for figs**.
14 And he said to it, "May no one ever eat fruit from you again."
And his disciples heard it.

* temple [témpl] ⑱ 성전.

** fig [fig] ⑱ 무화과.

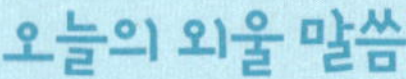

Hosanna! Blessed is he who comes in the name of the Lord!
Blessed is the coming kingdom of our father David!
Hosanna in the highest! (11:9b-10)

호산나 찬송하리로다 주의 이름으로 오시는 이여
찬송하리로다 오는 우리 조상 다윗의 나라여
가장 높은 곳에서 호산나 하더라.

하루 한 문장, 생각 쓰기

오늘 본문을 쓰면서 깨달은 지혜, 새롭게 다짐한 점,
떠오른 생각 등을 자유롭게 적어 보세요.

DAY 21

DATE . . .

Mark 11

Jesus Cleanses the Temple

15 And they came to Jerusalem. And he entered the temple and
began to drive out those who sold and those who bought in
the temple, and he overturned the tables of the money-changers
and the seats of those who sold pigeons.

16 And he would not allow anyone to carry anything through
the temple.

17 And he was teaching them and saying to them, "Is it not written,
'My house shall be called a house of prayer for all the nations'?
But you have made it a den of robbers."

18 And the chief priests and the scribes heard it and were seeking
a way to destroy him, for they feared him, because all the crowd
was astonished at his teaching.

19 And when evening came they went out of the city.

The Lesson from the Withered Fig Tree

20 As they passed by in the morning, they saw the fig tree withered
away to its roots.

21 And Peter remembered and said to him, "Rabbi, look! The fig tree
that you cursed has withered."

22 And Jesus answered them, "Have faith in God.
23 Truly, I say to you, whoever says to this mountain, 'Be taken up
and thrown into the sea,' and does not doubt* in his heart,
but believes that what he says will come to pass, it will be done
for him.
24 Therefore I tell you, whatever you ask in prayer, believe that you
have received it, and it will be yours.
25 And whenever you stand praying, forgive, if you have anything
against anyone, so that your Father also who is in heaven may
forgive you your trespasses**."

The Authority of Jesus Challenged

27 And they came again to Jerusalem. And as he was walking in
the temple, the chief priests and the scribes and the elders came
to him,
28 and they said to him, "By what authority are you doing these
things, or who gave you this authority to do them?"
29 Jesus said to them, "I will ask you one question; answer me,
and I will tell you by what authority I do these things.
30 Was the baptism of John from heaven or from man? Answer me."
31 And they discussed it with one another, saying, "If we say, 'From
heaven,' he will say, 'Why then did you not believe him?'
32 But shall we say, 'From man'?"—they were afraid of the people,
for they all held that John really was a prophet.

* doubt [daut] ⓜ 의심. ⓢ 의심하다.
** trespass [tréspəs] ⓜ 죄. ⓢ 무단 침입하다.

33 So they answered Jesus, "We do not know." And Jesus said to
them, "Neither will I tell you by what authority I do these things."

오늘의 외울 말씀

And whenever you stand praying, forgive,
if you have anything against anyone,
so that your Father also who is in heaven may forgive you
your trespasses. (11:25)

서서 기도할 때에 아무에게나 혐의가 있거든 용서하라
그리하여야 하늘에 계신 너희 아버지께서도
너희 허물을 사하여 주시리라 하시니라.

하루 한 문장, 생각 쓰기

오늘 본문을 쓰면서 깨달은 지혜, 새롭게 다짐한 점,
떠오른 생각 등을 자유롭게 적어 보세요.

DAY 22

DATE . . .

Mark 12

The Parable of the Tenants

1 And he began to speak to them in parables.
"A man planted a vineyard and put a fence around it and dug
a pit for the winepress and built a tower, and leased it to tenants
and went into another country.
2 When the season came, he sent a servant to the tenants to get
from them some of the fruit of the vineyard.
3 And they took him and beat him and sent him away empty-
handed.
4 Again he sent to them another servant, and they struck him on
the head and treated him shamefully.
5 And he sent another, and him they killed. And so with many
others: some they beat, and some they killed.
6 He had still one other, a beloved son. Finally he sent him to
them, saying, 'They will respect my son.'
7 But those tenants said to one another, 'This is the heir. Come,
let us kill him, and the inheritance will be ours.'
8 And they took him and killed him and threw him out of
the vineyard.

9 What will the owner of the vineyard do? He will come and
destroy the tenants and give the vineyard to others.
10 Have you not read this Scripture: "'The stone that the builders
rejected has become the cornerstone;
11 this was the Lord's doing, and it is marvelous in our eyes'?"
12 And they were seeking to arrest him but feared the people,
for they perceived that he had told the parable against them.
So they left him and went away.

Paying Taxes to Caesar

13 And they sent to him some of the Pharisees and some of
the Herodians, to trap him in his talk.
14 And they came and said to him, "Teacher, we know that you
are true and do not care about anyone's opinion. For you are
not swayed* by appearances, but truly teach the way of God. Is
it lawful to pay taxes to Caesar, or not? Should we pay them, or
should we not?"
15 But, knowing their hypocrisy**, he said to them, "Why put me to
the test? Bring me a denarius and let me look at it."
16 And they brought one. And he said to them, "Whose likeness and
inscription*** is this?" They said to him, "Caesar's."
17 Jesus said to them, "Render to Caesar the things that are Caesar's,
and to God the things that are God's." And they marveled at him.

* sway [swei] ⓜ 동요. 영향. ⓓ 흔들리다. 기울다.

** hypocrisy [hipákrəsi] ⓜ 위선. 가장.

*** inscription [inskrípʃən] ⓜ (책, 금석에) 적힌 글. 말. 비문.

오늘의 외울 말씀

Jesus said to them, "Render to Caesar the things that are Caesar's, and to God the things that are God's." (12:17a)

이에 예수께서 이르시되 가이사의 것은 가이사에게, 하나님의 것은 하나님께 바치라 하시니.

하루 한 문장, 생각 쓰기

오늘 본문을 쓰면서 깨달은 지혜, 새롭게 다짐한 점,
떠오른 생각 등을 자유롭게 적어 보세요.

DAY 23

DATE . . .

Mark 12

The Sadducees Ask About the Resurrection

18 And Sadducees came to him, who say that there is no
resurrection. And they asked him a question, saying,

19 "Teacher, Moses wrote for us that if a man's brother dies and
leaves a wife, but leaves no child, the man must take the widow
and raise up offspring* for his brother.

20 There were seven brothers; the first took a wife, and when he died
left no offspring.

21 And the second took her, and died, leaving no offspring.
And the third likewise.

22 And the seven left no offspring. Last of all the woman also died.

23 In the resurrection, when they rise again, whose wife will she be?
For the seven had her as wife."

24 Jesus said to them, "Is this not the reason you are wrong,
because you know neither the Scriptures nor the power of God?

25 For when they rise from the dead, they neither marry nor are
given in marriage, but are like angels in heaven.

* offspring [ɔfspriŋ] ⓜ 자식.

26 And as for the dead being raised, have you not read in the book
of Moses, in the passage about the bush*, how God spoke to him,
saying, 'I am the God of Abraham, and the God of Isaac,
and the God of Jacob'?
27 He is not God of the dead, but of the living. You are quite wrong."

The Great Commandment

28 And one of the scribes came up and heard them disputing with
one another, and seeing that he answered them well, asked him,
"Which commandment is the most important of all?"
29 Jesus answered, "The most important is, 'Hear, O Israel: The Lord
our God, the Lord is one.
30 And you shall love the Lord your God with all your heart and
with all your soul and with all your mind and with all your
strength.'
31 The second is this: 'You shall love your neighbor as yourself.'
There is no other commandment greater than these."
32 And the scribe said to him, "You are right, Teacher. You have
truly said that he is one, and there is no other besides him.
33 And to love him with all the heart and with all the understanding
and with all the strength, and to love one's neighbor as oneself,
is much more than all whole burnt offerings** and sacrifices."
34 And when Jesus saw that he answered wisely, he said to him,
"You are not far from the kingdom of God." And after that no
one dared to ask him any more questions.

* bush [buʃ] ⑲ 떨기나무.

** burnt offering ⑲ 번제물.

Whose Son Is the Christ?

35 And as Jesus taught in the temple, he said, "How can the scribes
say that the Christ is the son of David?

36 David himself, in the Holy Spirit, declared, "'The Lord said to my
Lord, "Sit at my right hand, until I put your enemies under your
feet."'

37 David himself calls him Lord. So how is he his son?"
And the great throng heard him gladly.

Beware of the Scribes

38 And in his teaching he said, "Beware of the scribes, who like to
walk around in long robes and like greetings in the marketplaces

39 and have the best seats in the synagogues and the places of honor
at feasts,

40 who devour widows' houses and for a pretense make long prayers.
They will receive the greater condemnation.*"

The Widow's Offering

41 And he sat down opposite the treasury** and watched the people
putting money into the offering box. Many rich people put in
large sums.

42 And a poor widow came and put in two small copper coins,
which make a penny.

* condemnation [kàndemnéiʃən] ⑲ 비난. 유죄 판결.

** treasury [tréʒəri] ⑲ 헌금함.

43 And he called his disciples to him and said to them, "Truly, I say
to you, this poor widow has put in more than all those who are
contributing to the offering box.
44 For they all contributed out of their abundance*, but she out of
her poverty has put in everything she had, all she had to live on."

* abundance [əbʌndəns] ⑱ 풍부. 부유.

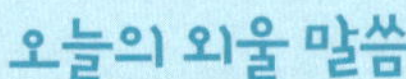

The most important is,
… 'you shall love the Lord your God with all your heart
and with all your soul and with all your mind
and with all your strength.'
The second is this: 'You shall love your neighbor as yourself.' (12:29-31)

첫째는 이것이니…네 마음을 다하고 목숨을 다하고 뜻을 다하고 힘을 다하여
주 너의 하나님을 사랑하라 하신 것이요
둘째는 이것이니 네 이웃을 네 자신과 같이 사랑하라 하신 것이라.

하루 한 문장, 생각 쓰기

오늘 본문을 쓰면서 깨달은 지혜, 새롭게 다짐한 점,
떠오른 생각 등을 자유롭게 적어 보세요.

DAY 24

DATE . . .

Mark 13

Jesus Foretells Destruction of the Temple

1 And as he came out of the temple, one of his disciples said to
him, "Look, Teacher, what wonderful stones and what wonderful
buildings!"

2 And Jesus said to him, "Do you see these great buildings?
There will not be left here one stone upon another that will not
be thrown down."

Signs of the End of the Age

3 And as he sat on the Mount of Olives opposite the temple,
Peter and James and John and Andrew asked him privately,

4 "Tell us, when will these things be, and what will be the sign
when all these things are about to be accomplished?"

5 And Jesus began to say to them, "See that no one leads you astray.

6 Many will come in my name, saying, 'I am he!' and they will lead
many astray.

7 And when you hear of wars and rumors of wars, do not be
alarmed. This must take place, but the end is not yet.

8 For nation will rise against nation, and kingdom against
kingdom. There will be earthquakes in various places; there will
be famines. These are but the beginning of the birth pains.
9 "But be on your guard. For they will deliver you over to councils,
and you will be beaten in synagogues, and you will stand before
governors and kings for my sake*, to bear witness before them.
10 And the gospel must first be proclaimed to all nations.
11 And when they bring you to trial and deliver you over, do not be
anxious beforehand** what you are to say, but say whatever is given
you in that hour, for it is not you who speak, but the Holy Spirit.
12 And brother will deliver brother over to death, and the father his
child, and children will rise against parents and have them put to
death.
13 And you will be hated by all for my name's sake. But the one who
endures to the end will be saved.

* sake [seik] ⓜ 동기. 이익. 목적. 이유.

** beforehand [bifɔ́:rhænd] ⓟ 사전에. …전에 미리.

오늘의 외울 말씀

And when they bring you to trial and deliver you over,
do not be anxious beforehand what you are to say,
but say whatever is given you in that hour,
for it is not you who speak, but the Holy Spirit. (13:11)

사람들이 너희를 끌어다가 넘겨 줄 때에 무슨 말을 할까 미리 염려하지 말고
무엇이든지 그 때에 너희에게 주시는 그 말을 하라
말하는 이는 너희가 아니요 성령이시니라.

하루 한 문장, 생각 쓰기

오늘 본문을 쓰면서 깨달은 지혜, 새롭게 다짐한 점,
떠오른 생각 등을 자유롭게 적어 보세요.

DAY 25

DATE . . .

Mark 13

The Abomination of Desolation

14 "But when you see the abomination of desolation standing where
he ought not to be (let the reader understand), then let those who
are in Judea flee to the mountains.

15 Let the one who is on the housetop not go down, nor enter his
house, to take anything out,

16 and let the one who is in the field not turn back to take his cloak.

17 And alas for women who are pregnant and for those who are
nursing infants in those days!

18 Pray that it may not happen in winter.

19 For in those days there will be such tribulation as has not been
from the beginning of the creation that God created until now,
and never will be.

20 And if the Lord had not cut short the days, no human being
would be saved. But for the sake of the elect, whom he chose,
he shortened the days.

21 And then if anyone says to you, 'Look, here is the Christ!' or 'Look,
there he is!' do not believe it.

22 For false christs and false prophets will arise and perform signs and wonders, to lead astray, if possible, the elect*.

23 But be on guard; I have told you all things beforehand.

The Coming of the Son of Man

24 "But in those days, after that tribulation, the sun will be darkened, and the moon will not give its light,

25 and the stars will be falling from heaven, and the powers in the heavens will be shaken.

26 And then they will see the Son of Man coming in clouds with great power and glory.

27 And then he will send out the angels and gather his elect from the four winds, from the ends of the earth to the ends of heaven.

The Lesson of the Fig Tree

28 "From the fig tree learn its lesson: as soon as its branch becomes tender and puts out its leaves, you know that summer is near.

29 So also, when you see these things taking place, you know that he is near, at the very gates.

30 Truly, I say to you, this generation will not pass away until all these things take place.

31 Heaven and earth will pass away, but my words will not pass away.

* elect [ilékt] ⓜ 하나님의 선택을 받은 사람들.

No One Knows That Day or Hour

32 "But concerning that day or that hour, no one knows, not even
the angels in heaven, nor the Son, but only the Father.
33 Be on guard, keep awake. For you do not know when the time
will come.
34 It is like a man going on a journey, when he leaves home and puts
his servants in charge, each with his work, and commands
the doorkeeper to stay awake.
35 Therefore stay awake—for you do not know when the master of
the house will come, in the evening, or at midnight, or when
the rooster crows, or in the morning—
36 lest he come suddenly and find you asleep.
37 And what I say to you I say to all: Stay awake."

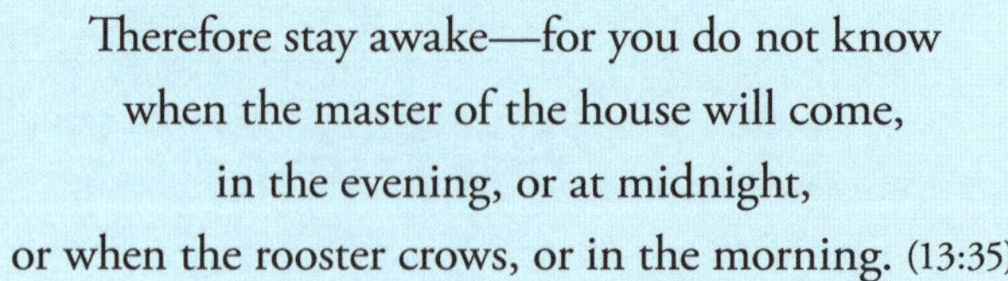

오늘의 외울 말씀

Therefore stay awake—for you do not know
when the master of the house will come,
in the evening, or at midnight,
or when the rooster crows, or in the morning. (13:35)

그러므로 깨어 있으라 집 주인이 언제 올는지 혹 저물 때일는지, 밤중일는지,
닭 울 때일는지, 새벽일는지 너희가 알지 못함이라.

하루 한 문장, 생각 쓰기

오늘 본문을 쓰면서 깨달은 지혜, 새롭게 다짐한 점,
떠오른 생각 등을 자유롭게 적어 보세요.

DAY 26

DATE . . .

Mark 14

The Plot to Kill Jesus

1 It was now two days before the Passover and the Feast of
Unleavened Bread. And the chief priests and the scribes were
seeking how to arrest him by stealth and kill him,
2 for they said, "Not during the feast, lest there be an uproar from
the people."

Jesus Anointed at Bethany

3 And while he was at Bethany in the house of Simon the leper,
as he was reclining at table, a woman came with an alabaster flask
of ointment of pure nard, very costly, and she broke the flask and
poured it over his head.
4 There were some who said to themselves indignantly, "Why was
the ointment wasted like that?
5 For this ointment could have been sold for more than three
hundred denarii and given to the poor." And they scolded her.
6 But Jesus said, "Leave her alone. Why do you trouble her?
She has done a beautiful thing to me.
7 For you always have the poor with you, and whenever you want,
you can do good for them. But you will not always have me.

8 She has done what she could; she has anointed my body
beforehand for burial*.

9 And truly, I say to you, wherever the gospel is proclaimed in
the whole world, what she has done will be told in memory of
her."

Judas to Betray Jesus

10 Then Judas Iscariot, who was one of the twelve, went to the chief
priests in order to betray him to them.

11 And when they heard it, they were glad and promised to give him
money. And he sought an opportunity to betray him.

The Passover with the Disciples

12 And on the first day of Unleavened Bread, when they sacrificed
the Passover lamb, his disciples said to him, "Where will you have
us go and prepare for you to eat the Passover**?"

13 And he sent two of his disciples and said to them, "Go into
the city, and a man carrying a jar of water will meet you.
Follow him,

14 and wherever he enters, say to the master of the house,
'The Teacher says, Where is my guest room, where I may eat
the Passover with my disciples?'

15 And he will show you a large upper room furnished and ready;
there prepare for us."

* burial [bériəl] ⑱ 장례.

** Passover [pæsouvər] ⑱ 유월절.

16 And the disciples set out and went to the city and found it just as
he had told them, and they prepared the Passover.

17 And when it was evening, he came with the twelve.

18 And as they were reclining at table and eating, Jesus said, "Truly, I
say to you, one of you will betray me, one who is eating with me."

19 They began to be sorrowful* and to say to him one after another,
"Is it I?"

20 He said to them, "It is one of the twelve, one who is dipping
bread into the dish with me.

21 For the Son of Man goes as it is written of him, but woe to that
man by whom the Son of Man is betrayed! It would have been
better for that man if he had not been born."

Institution of the Lord's Supper

22 And as they were eating, he took bread, and after blessing it broke
it and gave it to them, and said, "Take; this is my body."

23 And he took a cup, and when he had given thanks he gave it to
them, and they all drank of it.

24 And he said to them, "This is my blood of the covenant**, which is
poured out for many.

25 Truly, I say to you, I will not drink again of the fruit of the vine
until that day when I drink it new in the kingdom of God."

* sorrowful [sɑ́rəfəl] ⓗ 슬픈.

** covenant [kʌvənənt] ⓜ 언약. 약속. 계약.

Jesus Foretells Peter's Denial

26 And when they had sung a hymn, they went out to the Mount of
Olives.
27 And Jesus said to them, "You will all fall away, for it is written,
'I will strike the shepherd, and the sheep will be scattered.'
28 But after I am raised up, I will go before you to Galilee."
29 Peter said to him, "Even though they all fall away, I will not."
30 And Jesus said to him, "Truly, I tell you, this very night,
before the rooster crows twice, you will deny me three times."
31 But he said emphatically*, "If I must die with you, I will not deny
you." And they all said the same.

* emphatically [imfǽtikəli] ⊕ 강조하여, 단호히, 단연코.

오늘의 외울 말씀

And he said to them, "This is my blood of the covenant,
which is poured out for many." (14:24)

이르시되 이것은 많은 사람을 위하여 흘리는 나의 피 곧 언약의 피니라.

하루 한 문장, 생각 쓰기

오늘 본문을 쓰면서 깨달은 지혜, 새롭게 다짐한 점,
떠오른 생각 등을 자유롭게 적어 보세요.

DAY 27

DATE . . .

Mark 14

Jesus Prays in Gethsemane

32 And they went to a place called Gethsemane. And he said to his
disciples, "Sit here while I pray."

33 And he took with him Peter and James and John, and began to be
greatly distressed and troubled.

34 And he said to them, "My soul is very sorrowful, even to death.
Remain here and watch."

35 And going a little farther, he fell on the ground and prayed that,
if it were possible, the hour might pass from him.

36 And he said, "Abba, Father, all things are possible for you.
Remove this cup from me. Yet not what I will, but what you will."

37 And he came and found them sleeping, and he said to Peter,
"Simon, are you asleep? Could you not watch one hour?

38 Watch and pray that you may not enter into temptation.
The spirit indeed is willing, but the flesh is weak."

39 And again he went away and prayed, saying the same words.

40 And again he came and found them sleeping, for their eyes were
very heavy, and they did not know what to answer him.

41 And he came the third time and said to them, "Are you still
sleeping and taking your rest? It is enough; the hour has come.
The Son of Man is betrayed into the hands of sinners.
42 Rise, let us be going; see, my betrayer is at hand."

Betrayal and Arrest of Jesus

43 And immediately, while he was still speaking, Judas came, one of
the twelve, and with him a crowd with swords and clubs,
from the chief priests and the scribes and the elders.
44 Now the betrayer had given them a sign, saying, "The one I will
kiss is the man. Seize him and lead him away under guard."
45 And when he came, he went up to him at once and said, "Rabbi!"
And he kissed him.
46 And they laid hands on him and seized him.
47 But one of those who stood by drew his sword and struck
the servant of the high priest and cut off his ear.
48 And Jesus said to them, "Have you come out as against a robber,
with swords and clubs to capture me?
49 Day after day I was with you in the temple teaching, and you did
not seize me. But let the Scriptures be fulfilled."
50 And they all left him and fled.

A Young Man Flees

51 And a young man followed him, with nothing but a linen cloth
about his body. And they seized him,
52 but he left the linen cloth and ran away naked.

Jesus Before the Council

53 And they led Jesus to the high priest. And all the chief priests and
the elders and the scribes came together.
54 And Peter had followed him at a distance, right into the courtyard
of the high priest. And he was sitting with the guards and
warming himself at the fire.
55 Now the chief priests and the whole council were seeking
testimony against Jesus to put him to death, but they found none.
56 For many bore false witness* against him, but their testimony did
not agree.
57 And some stood up and bore false witness against him, saying,
58 "We heard him say, 'I will destroy this temple that is made with
hands, and in three days I will build another, not made with
hands.'"
59 Yet even about this their testimony did not agree.
60 And the high priest stood up in the midst and asked Jesus,
"Have you no answer to make? What is it that these men testify
against you?"
61 But he remained silent and made no answer. Again the high priest
asked him, "Are you the Christ, the Son of the Blessed?"
62 And Jesus said, "I am, and you will see the Son of Man seated at
the right hand of Power, and coming with the clouds of heaven."
63 And the high priest tore his garments and said, "What further**
witnesses do we need?

* witness [wítnis] ⓜ 목격자. ⓢ 목격하다.
** further [fə́ːrðər] ⓗ 더 이상의. 추가의.

64 You have heard his blasphemy. What is your decision?"
And they all condemned him as deserving death.
65 And some began to spit on him and to cover his face and to strike
him, saying to him, "Prophesy!" And the guards received him
with blows.

Peter Denies Jesus

66 And as Peter was below in the courtyard, one of the servant girls
of the high priest came,
67 and seeing Peter warming himself, she looked at him and said,
"You also were with the Nazarene, Jesus."
68 But he denied it, saying, "I neither know nor understand what
you mean." And he went out into the gateway and the rooster
crowed.
69 And the servant girl saw him and began again to say to
the bystanders*, "This man is one of them."
70 But again he denied it. And after a little while the bystanders
again said to Peter, "Certainly you are one of them, for you are
a Galilean."
71 But he began to invoke a curse on himself and to swear**, "I do
not know this man of whom you speak."
72 And immediately the rooster crowed a second time. And Peter
remembered how Jesus had said to him, "Before the rooster crows
twice, you will deny me three times." And he broke down and
wept.

* bystander [baistændər] ⓜ 구경꾼.
** swear [swɛər] ⓢ 맹세하다. 욕하다. 단언하다.

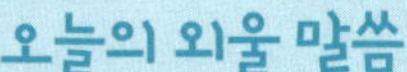

오늘의 외울 말씀

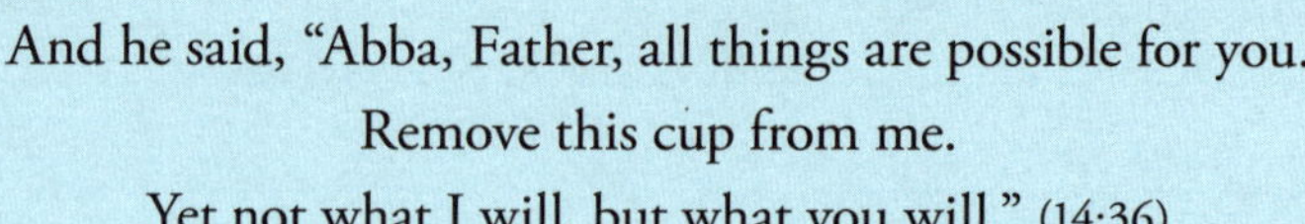

And he said, "Abba, Father, all things are possible for you.
Remove this cup from me.
Yet not what I will, but what you will." (14:36)

이르시되 아빠 아버지여 아버지께는 모든 것이 가능하오니
이 잔을 내게서 옮기시옵소서
그러나 나의 원대로 마시옵고 아버지의 원대로 하옵소서 하시고.

하루 한 문장, 생각 쓰기

오늘 본문을 쓰면서 깨달은 지혜, 새롭게 다짐한 점,
떠오른 생각 등을 자유롭게 적어 보세요.

DAY 28

DATE . . .

Mark 15

Jesus Delivered to Pilate

1 And as soon as it was morning, the chief priests held a consultation
with the elders and scribes and the whole council. And they bound
Jesus and led him away and delivered him over to Pilate.

2 And Pilate asked him, "Are you the King of the Jews?" And he
answered him, "You have said so."

3 And the chief priests accused* him of many things.

4 And Pilate again asked him, "Have you no answer to make?
See how many charges they bring against you."

5 But Jesus made no further answer, so that Pilate was amazed.

Pilate Delivers Jesus to Be Crucified

6 Now at the feast he used to release for them one prisoner for
whom they asked.

7 And among the rebels in prison, who had committed murder in
the insurrection, there was a man called Barabbas.

8 And the crowd came up and began to ask Pilate to do as he
usually did for them.

* accuse [əkjúːz] ⑧ 고발하다, 혐의를 제기하다.

9 And he answered them, saying, "Do you want me to release for
you the King of the Jews?"

10 For he perceived that it was out of envy that the chief priests had
delivered him up.

11 But the chief priests stirred up the crowd to have him release for
them Barabbas instead.

12 And Pilate again said to them, "Then what shall I do with the man
you call the King of the Jews?"

13 And they cried out again, "Crucify him."

14 And Pilate said to them, "Why? What evil has he done?" But they
shouted all the more, "Crucify him."

15 So Pilate, wishing to satisfy the crowd, released for them Barabbas,
and having scourged Jesus, he delivered him to be crucified.

Jesus Is Mocked

16 And the soldiers led him away inside the palace (that is,
the governor's headquarters), and they called together the whole
battalion.

17 And they clothed him in a purple cloak, and twisting together
a crown of thorns, they put it on him.

18 And they began to salute him, "Hail, King of the Jews!"

19 And they were striking his head with a reed and spitting on him
and kneeling down in homage to him.

20 And when they had mocked him, they stripped him of the purple
cloak and put his own clothes on him. And they led him out to
crucify him.

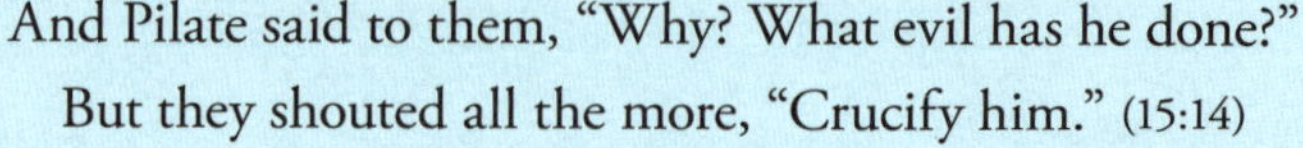

And Pilate said to them, “Why? What evil has he done?”
But they shouted all the more, “Crucify him.” (15:14)

빌라도가 이르되 어찌이냐 무슨 악한 일을 하였느냐 하니
더욱 소리 지르되 십자가에 못 박게 하소서 하는지라.

하루 한 문장, 생각 쓰기

오늘 본문을 쓰면서 깨달은 지혜, 새롭게 다짐한 점,
떠오른 생각 등을 자유롭게 적어 보세요.

DAY 29

DATE . . .

Mark 15

The Crucifixion

21 And they compelled a passerby, Simon of Cyrene, who was
coming in from the country, the father of Alexander and Rufus,
to carry his cross.

22 And they brought him to the place called Golgotha (which means
Place of a Skull).

23 And they offered him wine mixed with myrrh, but he did not
take it.

24 And they crucified him and divided his garments among them,
casting lots for them, to decide what each should take.

25 And it was the third hour when they crucified him.

26 And the inscription of the charge against him read, "The King of
the Jews."

27 And with him they crucified two robbers, one on his right and
one on his left.

29 And those who passed by derided him, wagging their heads and
saying, "Aha! You who would destroy the temple and rebuild it in
three days,

30 save yourself, and come down from the cross!"

31 So also the chief priests with the scribes mocked him to one
another, saying, "He saved others; he cannot save himself.

32 Let the Christ, the King of Israel, come down now from the cross
that we may see and believe." Those who were crucified* with him
also reviled him.

The Death of Jesus

33 And when the sixth hour had come, there was darkness over
the whole land until the ninth hour.

34 And at the ninth hour Jesus cried with a loud voice, "Eloi, Eloi,
lema sabachthani?" which means, "My God, my God, why have
you forsaken** me?"

35 And some of the bystanders hearing it said, "Behold, he is calling
Elijah."

36 And someone ran and filled a sponge with sour wine, put it on
a reed and gave it to him to drink, saying,
"Wait, let us see whether Elijah will come to take him down."

37 And Jesus uttered a loud cry and breathed his last.

38 And the curtain of the temple was torn in two, from top to
bottom.

39 And when the centurion***, who stood facing him, saw that in this
way he breathed his last, he said, "Truly this man was the Son of
God!"

* crucify [krúːsəfài] ⓢ 십자가에 매달아 죽이다.

** forsake [fərséik] ⓢ 버리다. 저버리다.

*** centurion [sentjúəriən] ⓜ 백부장.

40 There were also women looking on from a distance, among whom
were Mary Magdalene, and Mary the mother of James the younger
and of Joses, and Salome.
41 When he was in Galilee, they followed him and ministered to
him, and there were also many other women who came up with
him to Jerusalem.

Jesus Is Buried

42 And when evening had come, since it was the day of Preparation,
that is, the day before the Sabbath,
43 Joseph of Arimathea, a respected member of the council, who was
also himself looking for the kingdom of God, took courage* and
went to Pilate and asked for the body of Jesus.
44 Pilate was surprised to hear that he should have already died.
And summoning the centurion, he asked him whether he was
already dead.
45 And when he learned from the centurion that he was dead,
he granted the corpse to Joseph.
46 And Joseph bought a linen shroud, and taking him down,
wrapped him in the linen shroud and laid him in a tomb that had
been cut out of the rock. And he rolled a stone against
the entrance of the tomb.
47 Mary Magdalene and Mary the mother of Joses saw where he was
laid.

* courage [kə́:ridʒ] ⑲ 용기.

오늘의 외울 말씀

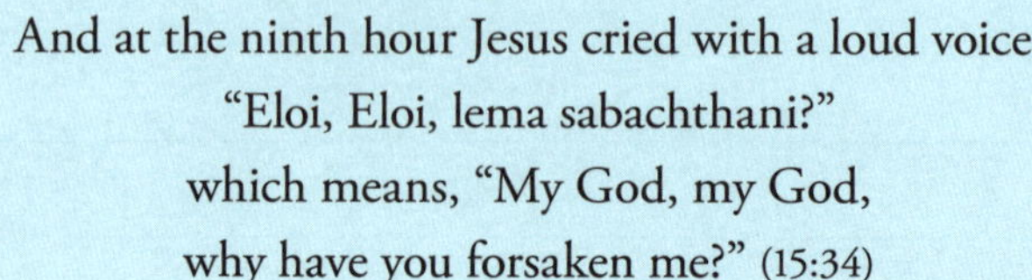

And at the ninth hour Jesus cried with a loud voice,
"Eloi, Eloi, lema sabachthani?"
which means, "My God, my God,
why have you forsaken me?" (15:34)

제구시에 예수께서 크게 소리 지르시되
엘리 엘리 라마 사박다니 하시니
이를 번역하면 나의 하나님, 나의 하나님
어찌하여 나를 버리셨나이까 하는 뜻이라.

하루 한 문장, 생각 쓰기

오늘 본문을 쓰면서 깨달은 지혜, 새롭게 다짐한 점,
떠오른 생각 등을 자유롭게 적어 보세요.

DAY 30

DATE . . .

Mark 16

The Resurrection

1 When the Sabbath was past, Mary Magdalene, Mary the mother
of James, and Salome bought spices, so that they might go and
anoint him.

2 And very early on the first day of the week, when the sun had
risen, they went to the tomb.

3 And they were saying to one another, "Who will roll away
the stone for us from the entrance of the tomb?"

4 And looking up, they saw that the stone had been rolled back—
it was very large.

5 And entering the tomb, they saw a young man sitting on the right
side, dressed in a white robe, and they were alarmed.

6 And he said to them, "Do not be alarmed. You seek Jesus of
Nazareth, who was crucified. He has risen; he is not here.
See the place where they laid him.

7 But go, tell his disciples and Peter that he is going before you to
Galilee. There you will see him, just as he told you."

8 And they went out and fled from the tomb, for trembling and
astonishment had seized them, and they said nothing to anyone,
for they were afraid.

[Some Of The Earliest Manuscripts Do Not Include 16:9–20.]

Jesus Appears to Mary Magdalene

9 [[Now when he rose early on the first day of the week, he appeared first to Mary Magdalene, from whom he had cast out seven demons.

10 She went and told those who had been with him, as they mourned* and wept.

11 But when they heard that he was alive and had been seen by her, they would not believe it.

Jesus Appears to Two Disciples

12 After these things he appeared in another form to two of them, as they were walking into the country.

13 And they went back and told the rest, but they did not believe them.

The Great Commission

14 Afterward he appeared to the eleven themselves as they were reclining at table, and he rebuked them for their unbelief and hardness of heart, because they had not believed those who saw him after he had risen.

15 And he said to them, "Go into all the world and proclaim the gospel to the whole creation.

16 Whoever believes and is baptized will be saved, but whoever does not believe will be condemned.

* mourn [mɔːrn] ⓢ 애도하다. 슬퍼하다.

17 And these signs will accompany* those who believe: in my name
they will cast out demons; they will speak in new tongues;
18 they will pick up serpents with their hands; and if they drink any
deadly poison, it will not hurt them; they will lay their hands on
the sick, and they will recover."
19 So then the Lord Jesus, after he had spoken to them, was taken
up into heaven and sat down at the right hand of God.
20 And they went out and preached everywhere, while the Lord
worked with them and confirmed the message by accompanying
signs.]]

* accompany [əkʌmpəni] ⓢ 따르다. 동반하다.

오늘의 외울 말씀

And he said to them, "Do not be alarmed.
You seek Jesus of Nazareth, who was crucified.
He has risen; he is not here.
See the place where they laid him." (16:6)

청년이 이르되 놀라지 말라
너희가 십자가에 못 박히신 나사렛 예수를 찾는구나
그가 살아나셨고 여기 계시지 아니하니라
보라 그를 두었던 곳이니라.

하루 한 문장, 생각 쓰기

오늘 본문을 쓰면서 깨달은 지혜, 새롭게 다짐한 점,
떠오른 생각 등을 자유롭게 적어 보세요.

사랑을 더하면 온전해집니다.

이 모든 것 위에 사랑을 더하라 이는 온전하게 매는 띠니라(골 3:14).

도서출판 사랑플러스는 이 땅의 모든 교회와 성도들을 섬기기 위해 국제제자훈련원이 설립한 출판 사역 기관입니다.

십대를 위한 마가복음 영어로 한 달 쓰기

초판 1쇄 인쇄 2022년 4월 6일
초판 1쇄 발행 2022년 4월 20일

엮은이 사랑플러스 편집부

펴낸이 오정현
펴낸곳 사랑플러스
등록번호 제2002-000032호(2002년 2월 15일)
주소 서울시 서초구 효령로 68길 98(서초동)
전화 02)3489-4300 **팩스** 02)3489-4329
이메일 dmipress@sarang.org

ISBN 979-11-88402-15-1 43230

※ 책값은 뒤표지에 있습니다. 잘못된 책은 구입하신 곳에서 교환해드립니다.